The Daily Life of a NYC Commuter

The comical things that happen on my commute to and from work

Alyse Landers

Cover design & illustrations by Rio

ISBN: 978-0-9970497-0-1

Dedication

To all my fellow commuters. Thank you for a wealth of unsolicited material.

.

Contents

Introduction

I never considered myself an author—or even a good writer. However, there comes a time in life when you realize you have a certain something to share with the world and there is an inner burning desire to put pen to paper that doesn't go away. Your story must be shared. If it hasn't happened to you yet then any given day could be the catalyst toward your writing career. I never thought it would or could happen to me, but there are some things that can't go unnoticed. For example, I give you "Santa Porn." Now if those two words don't get you going I don't know what will. It was on a December day just around Christmas, when I realized my stories were too good to keep all to myself. That would be selfish, wouldn't it? I mean when you are riding the train and on the seat across from you, someone is unashamedly engrossed in a book called, "Santa's Dirty Little Secret", you get intrigued. In addition to the title, the cover of the book flaunted a lurid illustration featuring the one and only Kris Cringle and a femme fatale with flaming red hair, crimson lipstick and do-me-now heels. She was giving Santa come hither eyes and a seductive stare. Now, tell me that wouldn't inspire you to start writing a book!

You do a lot of thinking and self-reflection on the train, and after getting over the initial shock that "Santa Porn" even exists, and the unsettling notion that people walk amongst us whose sexual choices somehow involve decking the halls with boughs of holly, I started thinking about how many truly bizarre and hysterical things have happened to me during my commute.

Like many people, I commute daily to and from work on the train. My commute is an hour long each way; that's two hours a day, 10 hours a week, 40 hours a month and 480 hours a year, which pales in comparison to the treks of other commuters, but after entertaining my friends and family for years with my train stories, I decided to make this year's 480 hours count for something.

I jotted down every story I heard or random thought I had this past year while commuting and I extracted the 30 best stories to include in this book. For you fellow NYC commuters, this book is comprised mostly of my Metro-North train experiences since that's my daily commute, with a handful of subway stories and Long Island Railroad stories in the mix. However, anyone who has commuted by public transportation should appreciate these stories regardless of which city, state or country you reside in. Even if you have never had the pleasure of experiencing public transportation before, you will still be able to appreciate the everyday humor in these stories.

This book is a collection of my real life experiences that have all REALLY happened on my daily commute to and from work. At points you might wonder, did this actually happen? And hand on heart I assure you it did, although names have been changed to protect the innocent. I hope you enjoy reliving these stories as much as I enjoyed witnessing and writing them. Truth is truly stranger than fiction—some things simply can't be made up.

~Alyse

Freakin' Chicken

Train rides teach me more lessons than any school, teacher or TV show. Yesterday's lesson: Don't mess with a woman and her chicken cravings. Seriously, DON'T. I can honestly say that I have heard a lot of crazy phone conversations on my daily rides to or from work. Break-ups, love confessions, weird stories about co-workers. You name it, I've heard it. But what I had the honor of witnessing yesterday on my way home was on a whole new level of crazy. I sat down next to a seemingly nice woman who even smiled at me (a rare sighting in NYC) and offered me some chewing gum. I had no idea what I was about to experience only a few moments later. I gladly accepted the gum and sat there chewing, tired but happy, thinking about nothing really when the lady's phone started ringing.

She answered, "Hey baaaaabe, how's your day?"

Still, I suspected nothing—nothing but maybe a longer conversation with her significant other about how much they loved each other and so on. Annoying, but bearable. Little did I know, oh so god-damn little.

"Soooo sweetheart, did you pick up the fried chicken we wanted for dinner?"

Her voice was so sweet; how could anyone be born with a voice like that and not be made completely out of sugar? My voice sounds a bit rough even when I try to be nice. I'm just not blessed in that way.

And then, out of nowhere, hitting me like a fist in the stomach. "YOU GOT WHAT? GRILLED CHICKEN? ARE YOU FREAKIN' KIDDING??"

I must have had an expression of pure horror on my face because I felt my face muscles immediately tightening up. I turned my head a little to see if it really still was the angel-voiced woman sitting next to me and not some demon craving fried chicken

(NOT GRILLED, FRIED!). Still not sure what had just happened, I couldn't move, staring at the not-so-angelic-voiced lady who obviously was just getting started.

"Grilled chicken, Stephen, you know I don't eat that. There's a reason we fry stuff, BECAUSE IT FREAKIN' TASTES BETTER! Seriously, are you really that stupid, Stephen? Did I really marry a guy who's not even smart enough to figure out the difference between GRILLED AND FRIED? IS IT REALLY THAT HARD, STEPHEN? You keep doing stuff like that, Stephen, every god damn day and I'm really getting sick of it and as a matter of fact I am really getting sick of you! You really can't do anything right, can you? Can you Stephen?"

My mind was blown. Poor Stephen really got served. If I hadn't been so scared, I would have thrown in something about grilled being the healthier option, maybe, just maybe, but let's be honest, I was sitting there shaking in my pants just listening to her verbally abuse Stephen.

"What are you trying to tell me? Are you trying to tell me I'm fat? Are you? Let's give that fat ugly girl some grilled chicken, 'cause she's already huge enough? Is that what you're thinking about me, while I work my ass off every day to please you and your stupid expectations? You disgust me Stephen, you really do. Our marriage is not worth anything to you, for Christ's sake, NOT EVEN SOME FRIED CHICKEN!"

With that she hung up on him and slammed her phone down into her lap. That's when Stephen realized his lovely wife wasn't too happy with his choice of dinner tonight. Remind you, I still wasn't able to move. There was only one other time I have heard this kind of emotional outburst over chicken. It was years ago. My sister was around 10, we were in the car and she kept asking my mom over and over again if she could have ice cream for dinner.

After about the 20th time of, "Can I have ice cream, can I have ice cream, can I have ice cream," my mom finally lost it and turned to her and said "WE'RE HAVING FREAKIN' CHICKEN FOR DINNER NOT ICE CREAM." I guess poultry can sometimes push people over the edge.

Anyway, back to the current chicken debacle. I tried to act casual like I hadn't just witnessed a horrifying conversation but a not so quiet voice within myself screamed: *Get away from her. She's hungry, and she won't get her fried chicken now, SO YOU BETTER RUN!* But I was paralyzed; all I could do was sit there and try not to make eye contact. After a few minutes passed I started to relax; it seemed as if the danger was over and things had gone back to normal. However, as fate would have it at the next stop, a guy walks in holding a box of fried chicken in his hands, sits down on the seat opposite her, and starts to indulge in it. Her eyes were completely fixated on it. I said a silent prayer. Not so much for myself, but for him.

Mailbox Mystery

There is no question about it, in this world that is ever changing you must stay up to date. Just when I have one of those days in which my faith in humanity is almost completely destroyed, the train makes me believe in mankind again. Like today, when I was riding the train back home from a day filled with unpleasant events (terrible meetings, grumpy clients, cut budgets etc.) and several cases of bad karma (no coffee, running out of black ink, and hitting "reply all" on a confidential matter). To say I was not in the best mood is an understatement; I was plain annoyed with the world today. It was a day that seemed like literally everything went wrong within 12 hours. How is that even possible? Aren't there some rules in the universe making sure at least

SOMETHING has to go right, even on the worst of days? Apparently not. So when I sat down on one of the last available seats next to two men who were in their mid-70s I didn't expect my luck to change. Lord knows I was prepared for anything (bad) that day. So when they started talking about what I'm about to tell you, imagine the surprise on my face.

"It's amazing, there's this mailbox, right down my street, you know. Doesn't look a bit special, maybe a little larger than the average mailbox you see around here, but let me tell you it is. . ."

The passion and excitement in this man's voice made me smile. He was talking about a mailbox as if it was the most incredible thing ever. I couldn't help but feel my mood lighten up.

"It's a community thing. Everyone in our neighborhood puts books in this mailbox and anyone is able to take them. We're all sharing, it's amazing. I have been going every other week for the past two years to pick up some new reads. You really can find anything you want in there, Joe! Cookbooks to romance to criminal novels! I especially love the crime books Joe; you know how much I love reading those."

Bless his heart, don't we all.

"But listen Joe, the other day, when I went there . . . I found something, something special, something that wasn't a book . . . look what I found in the mailbox!!"

He rummaged through his huge old leather bag for what felt like hours and then finally pulled out what looked like a small metal plate. He ran his hand lovingly over the back side of the unknown metal treasure and then delicately turned it over. It took me a few seconds to realize what it actually was—a Kindle!—both Joe and I couldn't believe it. With the excitement of someone seeing their newborn for the first time, he continued . . .

"I have touched some of the buttons and it seems to let you read any book you want, Joe! Can you imagine that?! Endless amounts of books of every genre, right at the touch of a button! Who would have thought that would have been possible back in our day? Clearly someone thought the neighborhood should stay up to date and decided to introduce the loyal readers to a piece of modern reading technology!"

Joe's friend couldn't believe his eyes. He sat there with his mouth agape just staring at it in all its

Kindle glory, for a few good minutes. Needless to say, Joe and his friend were absolutely amazed.

His friend cautiously and carefully picked up the e-book reader and examined it as if he were a Neanderthal first seeing fire and exclaimed "This device is right out of a Science Fiction movie!!"

Their amazement melted my heart. The rest of the train ride I watched their facial expressions of pure joy and excitement with each touch of a button. They continued handling it, turning it on and off, swiping pages and zooming in and out. These guys were Kindle naturals.

Showing Off the Goods

Trains connect people—in the weirdest and craziest ways, but they do. Like the other day, when I was on my way home from work, the universe worked its magic through the public transportation system and answered my prayers.

I had just finished the new collection for my jewelry company, "New Age Charm" some days earlier and was now on the hunt for a good photographer to take pictures to turn the collection into a photo series for my website, ads and catalogs. I'm sure you all know how it is having to lay the responsibility for something you worked your butt off creating, something you put so much time, energy and soul into, something that is just really, really important to you, into the hands of someone who's basically a stranger.

It feels like abandoning your baby. And I already felt like a bad mom to my jewelry pieces even though I hadn't even found someone I would remotely consider being able to live up to the task. I tend to get slightly overly dramatic about this type of stuff but I can't help it. My jewelry is my heart and soul and I would rather hide it forever in my closet than put it into what I consider *unworthy hands*.

As I was sitting on the train, caught up in my own little jewelry drama, I noticed a man sitting on the opposite seat, taking pictures with what looked to me like a fairly professional and expensive camera. This was a sign. Praise public transportation for never ceasing to surprise me! Camera guy (his name was Dave) and I started talking. I told him about my collection and the struggle to find a trustworthy and competent person for the jewelry shoot, he gave me his card, outing himself as a professional photographer. I told him I'd call him within the next few days to make an appointment. Just like that, a few minutes on the train had solved everything. I felt like the happiest person on earth and even smiled at the grumpy guy (always on the same train as me, always in a bad mood) when I got out at my station. Life was definitely good.

After some days had passed, I called Dave and we arranged a time and date for the shoot. He suggested doing it at this well-known park in my area right next to the gazebo. This has always been my favorite park growing up so I knew the exact area he was referring to. The location was perfect for the shoot. The gazebo overlooks the water giving it the right amount of rustic charm and the right amount of sophisticated flair. I was EXCITED. He seemed to be just as motivated and passionate about the whole thing as I was which is not a very common thing to find.

I honestly couldn't wait for the arranged date, a Saturday afternoon to come. I had spent the whole week freaking out about everything looking perfect, every piece being all shiny and ready to be set in the best light possible. I even asked my sister, one of my best friends as well as my mom to come with me to the shoot, not only for help modeling the pieces but also for moral support.

So there we were, four overly excited women with several bags of jewelry, me a ball of nerves, my mom chill as usual, my sister making me even more nervous and my best friend (not from the area) trying to find the address I had given her . . . typical. Lord knows how, but she eventually made it to the park and we all starting walking up the hill to the designated spot. We were a few feet away and I saw that Dave was already there waiting for us; camera all set up, big smile on his face; on the bench next to him what looked to be a pile of clothing. As we got closer and the pile of clothing came into full view I realized it was actually lingerie. Yes you read it correctly, LINGERIE.

Who would have guessed, my new buddy Dave was actually a pinup model photographer and therefore used to taking pictures of quite different kinda jewels if you know what I mean. I think I was standing there, holding onto my bags of jewelry for a good minute before I could even speak. Luckily, my mom showed no such signs of shyness and started checking out the bras and panties right away. "Look honey, I think the red one would look so good on you!" Bless her heart, there ain't nothing on this planet making my mom feel uncomfortable.

So there we were, standing there and part of me *really* wanted to just roll with it, showing off the goods, no holding back! However the other part of me, the rational part, thought about future employers and pictures of me in my undies on Google forever . . . so yeah, we did decide to keep our clothes on. It turns out Dave was actually really talented and we ended up getting what turned out to be amazing pictures. Lesson learned. Before you show off the jewels make sure you don't have to show off the goods.

Just Another Manic Monday

Monday morning again. There's nothing more exhilarating than commuting to the city when its -16° out, the ground is covered with slushy wintry slop and the wind chill factor convinces you you'd be warmer standing inside a meat locker. Nope, not too many things could beat this kind of fun.

Screw sleeping in and staying in your warm, comfortable bed. I would much rather stand outside with the cold chiseling its way through my bones waiting for Godot. Wouldn't you?

Okay, I'm being a bit of a drama queen, the train was 5 minutes late but it felt like a ba-billion! I got on the train, sat down, and instantly became one with all the other miserable working freakazoids. Black jackets, black hats, black scarves, black gloves. It was like a funeral parlor convention.

Miserable people slumped everywhere in various stages of consciousness from half awake to half dead. The guy sleeping next to me reeked of alcohol from the night before. Another guy looked like he might have expired. Still others blabbed a tad too loudly on their phones about their precious offspring's latest achievements.

"Yeah, Brad came home with a trophy twice his height for correctly spelling *diarrhea*. He's a chip-off the old block that one, and just turned five."

Some—Buddhist and non-Buddhist alike—seemed to be contemplating who they could have possibly offended in a previous life to deserve ending up in a dead-end job in the seventh circle of hell that we call the workplace.

And when the combined negative psychological weight of the cold, the prospect of another five-day's helping of drudgery and the joy of making every mile of your journey with the Happy Embalmers club threatens to crush you, there's always daydreaming.

There's the day dreaming of running your own business from your PJs. The worry of: can I get out of dinner plans with that nincompoop Natalie from the sales department that I never wanted to agree to anyway. Or maybe I could pick up and leave everything right now and jet off to Florida to bask in the sunshine, pick oranges by day and play cello by night. Moreover, of course, there is the recurring daydream of wishing your boss would spontaneously combust right before your eyes.

On this particular Monday I had three large bags with me. I hate carrying bags on the train. It's so uncomfortable. At first, they sit unobtrusively on the seat next to you. But as more people get on, you're forced to play bag chess. You move your bags from chair to chair until the inevitable end of the game when they all end up stacked high on your lap while you vow never to bring another bag with you again as long as you live. You ladies especially know what I'm talking about here. It's even worse on the days when you MUST put makeup on before you get to the office. To let your co-workers see your true colors may scar them for life and that image will be burned into their brain muscle.

As you sit there with the leaning Tower of Pisa on your lap, you somehow need to navigate through bag number one to find your makeup. Then you have to deal with the nearly impossible task of making yourself look human while not jabbing yourself in the eyeball with your mascara.

Right when things are all sorted, meaning the pile on your lap is in prime position, makeup is out and you have gotten into the perfect applying flow, who comes by to mess it all up — the pesky ticket collector. Doesn't he know it just took me 20 full minutes to get it all right! He chooses this, of all moments, to appear.

I am now forced to halt the application of my makeup to play a leading role in *Mission Impossible V: Ticket Hunt*. My heart races. I toss the makeup back into my bag as I nervously rifle through my large pocket book, fingers frantically grazing through every section of the bag for that stupid ticket.

The entire time, he is hovering overhead like a hawk about to dive in for the kill. You finally pull it out and after all that effort on your behalf, he gives it a 2-second look and off he goes. What an unappreciative troll! Not one iota of thanks was shown for all that effort! You feel as if you could have pulled out that random business card you stuck your gum in last night to satisfy that narcissistic ape.

Next, it's back to the Chiquita Banana balancing act on my lap. There's no way I was leaving that train without doing my other eye and the rest of my face. It's hard to be a woman on the train and after all, you want to at least show up for work not looking like a drunken circus clown.

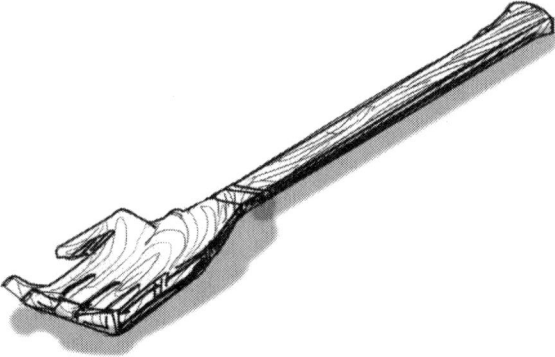

Backscratcher

Well here I was again, late as usual, running through the streets of the city trying to catch the train home to Queens to visit my parents. To avoid any further lateness and hearing my mom's voice saying "Really? Again?", I decided to hop on the subway to Penn-Station instead of taking the leisurely twenty-to-thirty minute walk from my office to Penn.

The walk to Penn Station from my office is twenty minutes if you have people in front of you that actually know how to walk in the city and thirty minutes if you get stuck behind a group of people that stop mid-walk to stare up at the big buildings, or stop dead in mid-walk to take a selfie. Stuff like this makes my blood boil. It's like a car abruptly stopping on the highway! Would anyone do that? No, I think not.

In an effort to eradicate thoughts of knocking down granny or acting out my running to the train recurring day dream of busting out into a superman costume, shooting down all the out of towners with kryptonite while flying over the masses to arrive just in time for my 6:29 pm train, I decided to run to the nearest subway station and reduce my Penn station commute time to about 5 minutes in length.

So there I was running down the steps of the subway frantically trying to catch the next train when I bumped into a man walking down the steps in front of me carrying a large stack of papers and what looked like a bunch of other odds and ends. Everything went flying out of his hands onto the dirty subway floor and that's when I saw it . . . just lying there on the ground . . . A LARGE WOODEN BACKSCRATCHER. I hadn't seen a backscratcher in twenty years. Now here I was face to face with someone who carted one around like it was a cell phone. I looked at the man with an expression that clearly said, "*Really?*"

The man who was obviously annoyed bent down to pick up his large wooden treasure and then turned around with a look of utter disgust and said "*What??? It's JUST a backscratcher.*"

Now I am not sure about you but never once have I traveled with a backscratcher in hand. No longer did I care about making my train; I hopped on the subway, sat back and smiled at the ridiculous situation. I guess you never know when you could have that sudden but urgent itch on your back in one of those doomed areas unreachable by the human hand. This man was certainly prepared for the unexpected.

Songs, Bongs and Thongs: The Subject Matter of Twenty-something Angst

At almost every stop along my hour journey to NYC, they clamber onto the train in groups of two or three, flaunting perfect nail polish and smelling like a hooker's handbag. Jennifer Aniston's personal makeup team could not produce such flawlessly made up faces.

Ten years from now they'll be sleepwalking on board with the rest of us, hair like birds' nests, wearing Walmart's own-brand of cosmetics that look like they've been applied with a palette knife during a power outage. For now though, they are full-time paid up members of Generation Y—fresh out of college, on their way to their first jobs in the city and looking cooler than a Kardashian on a red carpet.

Demonstrating the lethargy that only this age group can muster, they slump into seats facing each other as if this was the morning after and they've come straight from an all-night keg party.

Y's are easy to spot—the characteristics of the species being well known to anthropologists and fellow commuters alike. The most visual hint is the oversized sunglasses. These are worn with casual disregard for actual weather conditions (What's the forecast today? Snow? I'll wear my Ray-Bans. Monsoon rain? Shades, what else?).

Their sloppy posture makes you suspect they are incapable of speech, yet somehow they manage to air their concerns loudly enough for dozing commuters two train cars away to enjoy. You immediately find yourself longing for those happy days when your problems were as trivial as theirs—the days before rent hikes, the financial meltdown and 9/11.

Spontaneously, a Y feels compelled to share what, among their generation, passes for wisdom.

"OMG, like, I'm like, so tired. I was out until 1:00 am and I like, can't *believe* Samantha didn't show up. She, like, said she would be there and like, I'm so pissed off at her. She said she was coming and then I like, get a text saying she doesn't know if she can make it. Ugh! She's *always* doing this kind of stuff. Anyway, like, God I hate my job." The speaker is fluent in Jerry Springer Show English.

Their views are as unwavering as they are predictable. Whatever job they're traveling to, it'll be marginally better than share-cropping or smashing rocks on a chain gang. Every job is the worst job in the solar system. Work is a four letter word. Work is just sooo annoying. Why does it have to disrupt the important things in life—like songs, bongs and thongs? This 9 to 5 existence leaves your typical Y with little time to plan their next beer pong tournament. It's an Orwellian nightmare.

As the train clicketty-clacks toward its destination the conversation drifts toward the slightly less than riveting events of the previous weekend. These tales are low on verifiable facts and high on sexual innuendo. No attempts are made to keep this information hush-hush, even though they and their fellow passengers are packed tighter in the car than dancers in the mosh pit at a Megadeath concert.

Who slept with whom and why? Or didn't and why not? What happened with Eric—or was it Kyle? Can you *believe* that Bryan is dating married women—sometimes two at a time, with a third in reserve? And finally—hold the front page—isn't Samantha such a *bitch* (pronounced in two syllables: *Bee-hatch*).

To evidence exactly what Eric said over the weekend, cell phones pass back and forth in a music-less version of hot potato. The revealed dialog is mind-numbing enough to glaze the eyes on a ventriloquist's dummy.

"Hey you, hi."

"What are you up to?"

"Not much, you?"

Death of a Salesman this ain't

A new conversation re-kindles from the ashes of the previous Letterman-quality exchange. "And then I didn't answer because I didn't know what to say. What could I say? What would *you* have said? What does it all mean? Whatever, I am *sooo* tired."

"Anyway, my firm's laying off a bunch of people this week, but I don't even care, I may even enjoy it! The only thing is, I already have all my vacation time allotted for so that would suck. Besides that, I couldn't care less." *Mind you it's only February!*

It has been scientifically proven that this kind of language can cause those parts of the eavesdropper's brain that still consider life worth living, to vote for early retirement.

We are still several stops from our destination and already I feel like I simply have to disembark, even if that means climbing out a window and throwing myself onto the track. Twenty-something angst in twenty-first century America. Stop the train—no, wait—stop the *world*, I want to get off.

The Filthy Four

I admit it, I am no saint. In fact I can have a pretty dirty mind at times, and I think that's perfectly OK. Life is a lot funnier that way. But sometimes life itself simply outdoes me. Like recently, when innocent me was just on the train heading to work, not a single dirty thought on my mind.

It was basically all sunshine and rainbows up there. The virgin Mary herself couldn't have been purer. I had washed off all my sins during my morning shower routine and felt like a new born. I even checked my reflection in the windows to make sure my halo wasn't blinding the people around me. How unselfish of me, I know. Expecting people to jump

30

up for joy and scream, "Hallelujah", I was on the lookout for a free seat.

Even saints need a break sometimes, you know. As usual, spotting a free seat is a pretty hopeless endeavor on a typical morning heading to NYC but finally, before exhaustion won, I spotted a free seat right in the middle of a slightly funny looking group of elderly men. So I was like, what the h—whatever, better than having to stand for the whole ride, and I placed my oh-so innocent behind on the free spot right in the center of what looked like a veterans' meeting.

Prepared to be bombarded with stories about how good life used to be back in the old days and how incredibly impolite and reckless today's youth are, I leaned back, closed my eyes and gathered all of my patience to get through this train ride. But nothing. Silence. Deadly silence. I slowly opened one eye, just to check whether my not-so-fresh-anymore company was still breathing. They were; in fact all four of them were staring intently at a cell phone that was being passed around between each other. I couldn't help but smile. So cute, when old people try to get used to new technology.

This brought back memories of my granny trying to dial a number on her new smartphone (sad fact: hers was a way better model than mine). Or the one time my dad called me, totally out of it, desperation screaming in his voice. "Honey, I deleted the Internet!" Heroic me managed to "reanimate" the Internet back to life by relocating the explorer back onto the desktop—but my incredible computer skills are not the topic now.

My heart filled with sentimental thoughts, I glanced over at the phone screen. My innocence was wiped away immediately when I stared at a woman's naked ass twerking right in front of eyes, slowly opening her bra and . . . IT WAS 7.30am FOR GOD'S SAKE! Not that porn is only acceptable at a certain time, but COME ON. For a second I was torn between openly communicating my moral disgust and bursting out laughing. I decided to pretend I hadn't seen anything. But my thoughts for the rest of the train ride were definitely not about my granny anymore, let me tell you that.

Beer: It Isn't Just For Breakfast Anymore

It amazes me how so few people embrace an alcoholic beverage on the train ride home on a Friday. I look forward to this moment all week-long, it's a bit disappointing that I am the only sane person drinking in the train car.

It's typically me plus someone who looks to be homeless, but who am I to judge! So yes, I end up feeling like a bit of a lush-face but seriously, what is wrong with these people? It's Friday, the day that dreams are made of!

Today before boarding I thought to myself, I think I'll live on the edge and risk missing my train. As you can tell, I'm not much of a risk taker. I decide to make a mad-dash to one of the drink kiosks by the tracks and buy a glass of wine. With only two minutes to spare, the thought of buying a glass of wine of unrecognizable brand and mysterious origin quickly takes precedent over potentially missing my train. Frantically, I make the purchase and rush to make the train. To my own surprise and delight, I make it! I sit down and start enjoying. Thank goodness wine doesn't make that highly distracting popping noise like a can of beer when you open it. You can easily fly under the radar with wine, not so much though when it's two-beer Friday. Two-beer Friday's are reserved for those extra-long miserable work weeks.

On these special Friday's, I'll sit down and if my two cans are exposed—yes, we are *still* talking about beer here—there's an immediate stare down. All eyes on me—*Look, she has not one, but two cans of beer. My goodness; she is a wild raging alcoholic!* Then it's straight back to *The NY Times*, checking emails and texts about what's for dinner. The two-can beer drinking woman soon becomes a memory.

That is *until* it's time to pop open beer #2 and the popping noise of the can seems to ricochet through everyone's skull bone. It's as if, in that moment, I am Tarzan and I have just made a primal jungle yell rearing the heads of all animals. The folks look up—

Could it be? Could it truly be that she is drinking a second beer? Yes! Yesss! Look at that senseless and shameless beer guzzling hot chic! Okay, I threw in the "hot" part . . . there has to be some benefit to writing your own book.

It's a bit annoying that I have to be subjected to judgment while I am just minding my own beer loving business. They really need to find a way to quiet down these beer cans. It broadcasts to the entire world—*WARNING: someone is about to consume an alcoholic beverage.* Maybe they could put a muffler on it. Or wait; I got it! There should be beer juice boxes! Using the exact same packaging as the juice boxes we all enjoyed in elementary school, it would have a little straw on the back, and voilà—quiet beer container! This way, you could chug one down surreptitiously and no one would question why a grown adult is getting exponentially happier drinking so much apple juice.

Now most folks would feel a sense of shame in this Friday evening habit, feeling a slew of eyeballs on you and your canned cargo. You can almost hear their innermost monologue, and it goes something like this—*look at that poor women—she probably got fired today, or got dumped, or maybe she wasn't breastfed, or something else tragic most likely happened early in life.*

But no, I just have the amazing ability to house two 16 oz. cans of beer in a one-hour journey. And while we are on the topic of my amazing abilities, I think I really am on to something with the beer juice boxes. Once I have made my fortune and I am asked "How did you ever dream up such a product?" answer, "my love for beer, the Metro North and a wild imagination due to too much commuting time." Yes, ladies and gents, I believe we have a winner. Damon John get ready because *Shark Tank* here I come!

Handsome Golf Shoes

We all have our secrets. Some of them are darker than others, though. And some, well . . . some are just very special. Like the secret I had the honor to overhear during my train ride home from work today. I plopped down on the first seat I saw facing two men in their mid-40s. They looked like they had just made a good amount of money on Wall Street selling worthless shares to innocent but naive buyers. Maybe I am being too harsh but they certainly didn't look like the most likable human beings on that train. They had that whole look going, you know the look I'm talking about, the look that only men that are trying to recapture their youth can muster. The kind of look where you know they are trying way too hard. Spiked up hair, slim fit shirts, suit jackets that are a bit too tight coupled with fancy pocket squares and last but not least the Ray-Ban Aviators . . . on a rainy day.

The topic of their conversation didn't help either. They were having a lively discussion about golf and how obsessed they were with the sport. Call me ignorant but I never quite got golf. What is it that people are so attracted by? I guess you could question any sport in that way, but hitting a small plastic ball with a way too expensive metal stick is not my idea of great fun. I totally get football (muscular men running into each other), I can somehow understand baseball (the athletic version of a hit and run), but golf . . . sorry folks but golf is beyond me.

Guy #1 and his clone seemed to however feel quite differently about that. I started zoning out from their conversation as they went on and on about how tactical this and that player was, how well developed their own skills on the green had become thanks to their new instructor (shout-out to José, you're doing a great job man!) and how difficult it is to find the right golf clothes. Apparently the right attire plays a central role in this nebulous golf universe.

"The pants, they need to have the exact right fit. I can't play in pants that don't fit right, Andrew, I just physically can't." Andrew nodded in total agreement. I rolled my eyes.

Just when I was about to get my iPod out of my bag and put my headphones on, Andrew started saying something that made me want to listen to their so far boring conversation just a tiny bit longer. "Handsome golf shoes." I never heard someone describe anything in that way before.

Then I kept hearing him repeat it, "It's really all about the handsome golf shoes, Paul. I just can't get enough! Each pair is more handsome than the next."

Hearing him describe the shoes in this way was so completely laugh-out-loud funny to me I have never heard anyone describe an inanimate object as handsome. It then got even more interesting because Andrew said something about a confession he had to make and we all know confessions are the material drama is made from. And who doesn't want a little drama on the evening train, as long as it's not your own, of course. So back in the bag the iPod went and I was all ears again. Turns out Andrew had a *significant* passion for golf shoes.

"So a few years ago, I was lucky enough to get one of those special limited edition Nike pairs and I just don't know, Paul, but when I held that pair in my hands it felt so . . . it felt so good, you know? That's really when it started happening for me. They (the shoes, just FYI) are so important to me, every single pair. I started collecting them; it started out small just a new pair every few months." His friend nodded in agreement.

Then, Andrew continued, "It's like they each have their own personality and their own style! I feel like a different man depending on which pair I have on."

I couldn't see the face of Andrew's friend, but from his silence I am pretty sure he didn't know if his buddy was joking or not. And neither did I.

"The more handsome golf shoes I bought the more handsome golf shoes I wanted! They took over our entire garage. I convinced Carol to let me have my own area for my thirty or so handsome golf pairs. The thing is though, I kept wanting more and she kept getting increasingly upset every time I brought a new pair home. She told me I have a problem! She called it an obsession, can you believe that!? It's only a hobby; I don't know what the big deal is! She told me to just stick with what I have, that thirty pairs of golf shoes are more than enough for any human being. The thing is, it's just not enough for me; every time I see a new pair, I literally can't help but buy them. If I don't buy them right away, then all I do is think about them until I buy them. I mean they are handsome freaking golf shoes! The thing is,

Paul, Carol cannot find out about any of this. She would KILL me if she knew that I was buying more pairs. You know how mean she can get. You saw how she yelled at that poor maître d' when he didn't have our table ready in 10 minutes flat last month and that's just one of many outbursts."

"So the fact of the matter is I am now up to 83 precious pairs of handsome golf shoes and I have to hide ALL of them from Carol. So I bought this storage unit to keep them one town over. I'm thinking of buying another unit, because there's simply not enough space to display them all the way I want to. I can't just keep them in the boxes and pile them all up! Carol will kill me if she ever finds out. But be honest, Paul, it's not that bad, is it?"

Paul decided to be a good friend and helplessly shrug his shoulders while the expression on his face clearly screamed ARE YOU OUT OF YOUR MIND, BUDDY? But Andrew ignored his friend's horrified facial expression and kept giving a detailed description of his favorite pairs. Just when I got up because the train was approaching my station, Andrew was showing Paul pictures of possible new purchases on his phone. Poor Andrew; things were not looking good for him in terms of getting rid of his obsession any time soon. "Look at this pair—oh my, such handsome golf shoes; I mean look at the stitching and the leather. Paul, oh god, look at that leather!"

Fries, Anyone?

In case you haven't noticed yet, it is one's responsibility as a modern human being to be as fit and as good looking as possible. Otherwise, we're offensive and perhaps even a threat to our well-functioning society. Not being fit is simply not acceptable! At least that's what all the ads, magazines and TV-shows tell us. Get fit or die trying! If you don't look like one of those photo-shopped pictures of perfection we get bombarded with every day, *you clearly failed in life.* Simple as that. And I'm not saying it isn't important to be healthy or take care of your body, because it clearly is. I'm saying that society's goals and expectations of perfection are ridiculous. Even more ridiculous is the way they are forced upon us.

Just to prove that I'm not alone in my thinking, let me tell you about Susan, my new favorite human. I met her when I was riding the train home from work last week (actually, now that I think about it, I've met most of my favorite people on train . . . it's an interesting pattern in my life). She was sitting with a man on the seats opposite me. They were both in their early 40s and obviously had known each other for quite some time. I concluded they were either great friends or related in some way—it was hard to tell. I figured that out because Susan offered him one of her fries. And seriously, you wouldn't give up that crispy delicacy to just anyone. That moment of kindness with that single offered fry started a conversation I couldn't help but overhear. Well, actually I actively listened because, you know . . . it was about fries. Who wouldn't have found that fascinating?

"You have to start doing something for your body instead of filling it with junk like that Susan."

There we go. Mister 'I-know-exactly-what's-best-for-you-and-I-have-no-problem-discussing-it-here-on-a-train-filled-with-random-people' was just getting started. "Look at you! Is this really what you want for yourself?" *Bam*. He really had a way of giving it to her straight. If this was me, I would have punched him out at that point, but Susan was surprisingly cool, calm and collected. Talk about grounded people.

"I took a 30-minute walk today, John. Are you happy now?" Casually three more fries wandered into her mouth. I loved her already.

"It's not just exercise, Susan. We talked about that. You need to change your diet, I'm telling you!" He went on talking about some new version paleo diet he had just discovered. 'Paleo 2.0' or something like that. Susan was still completely unimpressed and unbothered, and continued to munch away.

"You really can't tell me that you actually feel good looking like this? I mean, GOOD LORD, you're fat, Susan!" At that point he pulled some brochure out of his bag and kept waving it in Susan's face. God, how could she just take this? I was seriously offended and he wasn't even talking to me.

"Let me have a look at that, John." Susan grabbed the brochure and for a second I thought, *What?* You're going to read this now? You were my hero, Susan. Why? *WHY?* But then in the most nonchalant way possible she slowly yet very accurately tore it up into little pieces and handed them back to a slightly alienated John. "That's what I think about your advice, John, but thanks anyway."

I had to hold back laughter so hard I thought I would explode. John's mouth stayed open for a small eternity before he finally collected himself and (can you believe this guy?) started a new attempt.

"You kept complaining why you aren't getting any dates from Match and eHarmony and maybe just maybe it's because these guys don't want to date a fat woman."

John had clearly crossed the line. Susan, being the hero I had known her to be, casually ate the last of her fries, stood up, gracefully gave John the middle finger and left her seat. John and I stared at each other. I couldn't help but smile.

"Was I . . . I don't know . . . do you think she?"

I shrugged my shoulders, grabbed the Snickers bar from my bag and said: "Should have taken the fry, John, should have taken it."

Aglets

Sometimes I can't help but reflect on the most random things. Like the importance of certain usually unnoticed things in our lives, these small aspects of everyday life we tend to overlook or just ignore because they seem so trivial. Be honest with yourself, you're guilty of doing it too, right? I mean, it's understandable, since our lives are so packed with information and stimulation it would be literally impossible to pay attention to everything we encounter on our daily quests for whatever it is we are striving for. And then you meet someone like Stan. *BAM*. Stan, I have to say, rocked my world. He turned it upside down. Stan was my hero that day I met him on the train. Because Stan reminded me that even the smallest, most common and overlooked things sometime need our time and attention.

For this whole story to make sense, we need to start at the very beginning, though. It all starts with aglets. I would love this to be a live stream right now because I sure as hell am curious to see your facial expression at this very moment. If it's anything like mine when I first heard Stan saying this word to his friend sitting next to him on the evening train home from work, it's a weird mixture of *what was that again you said?,* and *pretending you know the word so that people think you're smart!* Obviously I had never heard the word "aglet" before in my entire life. So Stan and his conversation with his friend came as a fundamental revelation to me, because I learned that aglets actually are the tiny plastic tips on the ends of shoelaces—that prevent the laces from frizzling and looking worn out in no time.

Stan, or rather the company Stan works for, saves the world from having to run around with terrible looking shoelaces, and the sad thing about that is clearly, 99.9% of this world's population doesn't even know what a great contribution Stan makes every day to basically all of our shoe-wearing society. As if that wasn't enough bad news for Stan already, overhearing his conversation I witnessed the many unexpected difficulties in producing a product nobody has ever heard of let alone paid any attention whatsoever to.

Turns out the aglets (I'll keep repeating that word until it irremovably is stuck in your subconscious mind and you'll never, ever forget it—my own personal tribute to Stan) were being produced in Thailand, not in the USA. A fact that kept causing Stan quite some trouble, since shipping didn't go as smoothly as expected.

"I ordered the light gray ones man, the light gray ones, explicitly, not dark gray, not black, not dotted, LIGHT GRAY. And what do they send me? Over 500 packets of NAVY BLUE ONES! I mean, can you believe that? IS THAT EVEN REAL?"

I got all worked up over the color-struggle myself. NAVY? *How could they*??? Feelings of anger and frustration built up in me and I was ready to give Stan a high five on correct color orders. Not only did the poor guy have to go his whole life without receiving any recognition for providing a necessary product everybody used without even noticing, he also had to deal with navy blue instead of light gray! And here I was, thinking that my day had been rough just because my colleague managed to spill a whole cup of coffee on my new blouse. My life was so damn easy compared to Stan's!

I really felt for him, as he sat there, pouring his heart out to his friend who couldn't do much but give him pitiful looks every now and then and say things like "Oh my" or "That's so tough though." The only thing that made me feel a little better was the fact that Stan got consolation; he had a good friend who was willing to listen to him complain about this crazy, frustrating shipment nightmare. Just before the train had reached my station, I sent an encouraging smile towards Stan, got up and was almost out of the train when I heard his friend say: "But man, what the hell are aglets?" Poor Stan. He'll remain forever misunderstood.

British Accents

British accents are basically a form of heaven on earth. I was on my way to work today and two elderly women I have never seen before sat to the left of me on the train. My head was bowed and I was leering at my cell phone because it had been almost five minutes since I last checked for messages.

A few moments later, the two strangers started a conversation. After a few words, I picked up on their British accent. You may be the dumbest person on Earth, but if you have that accent, you sound elegantly intelligent.

Absolutely everything that came out of their mouths sounded beautiful. The conversation began with the

ISIS crisis going into detail about the gruesome innocent slaughter. The detailed descriptions of this went on for quite some time. It was followed by how the Muslims are poisoning and ruining the world with their ideologies, how George W. got everyone into the Iraq mess and Obama got out too fast, and how all of this really doesn't matter because we are all going to die anyway.

You know, it was your typical upbeat morning conversation. Usually when I hear this kind of banter on the train, especially at 7-something in the morning, my earphones go right in. Who wants to be depressed before they even get to the office! Let work at least be the source of your depression. However, this morning was different. The tragedies and mismanagement of the world sounded like a magnificently orchestrated symphony to my ears. This was operatic brilliance to me! It clearly wasn't their context, but more the choreographed combination of accented words.

The subject matter quickly changed from ISIS to the captivating subject of fabric softener. Fabric softer and its proper application were discussed for at least fifteen minutes. I learned all about their laundry regimen, how often they do it, the size of their typical load, how far they have to walk to the laundromat, what they use for whites and what they use for colors. I was hanging on every word; the best brands to use, how it can even lead to soft skin, and last but not least they chuckled over the warning label of "Do Not Drink."

Who thinks about fabric softener once it is poured into the machine? Well, the entire conversation was all like a riveting gospel to me. Not only am I now a fan of theirs but I have never been more excited to get to Duane Reade and buy myself some fabric softener!

A Fishy Commuter Tale

I am not sure how it's possible, but people tend to look as miserable on Monday evening as they do on Monday morning. You would think everyone would be peppier since the first and suckiest day of the week is officially over. But no, there doesn't seem to be a change in the general demeanor of these train car trolls.

I guess it doesn't help that lately in the evenings the Metro North train cars have smelled like ripened, dead fish. Yes—dead, smelly, rotting, disgusting fish is what permeates your nostrils as soon as you step onboard. It's like a punch in the face!

Why this is an ongoing issue escapes me. Was there a secret meeting of the fish mongers held thirty minutes before us professional folks stepped on-board? Or, instead of this being a commuter train carrying people, was this recently used to transport the daily goods to the Fulton Fish Market? These days everyone is cutting down on costs, so it wouldn't surprise me if commuter trains were also starting to have a dual purpose. Let me remind you, this is happening about every other day for the past few weeks!

You would think that *someone*—perhaps the staff—or whosoever deals with train management or maintenance—would realize that the train cars smell like a pile of rotting fish. Rotting fish that has been baking in the sun all day and then smeared all over the seats and windows. Do the powers that be think this will increase the number of passengers? More likely than not this is another passive/aggressive MTA strike tactic! Those animals . . .

All of this aside, for some reason it gives me great comfort to think that instead of fish it's simply a dead body that has been rotting for weeks in some mysterious place on the train. I guess this at least makes the story more interesting, and in some ways, more bearable. Don't ask me why the presence of a dead body would be a more comforting thought than the presence of week old sushi filling the seats. I happen to love sushi, so perhaps I am giving myself the benefit of the doubt in order to preserve its innocence in the matter.

In retrospect I have to say, the one benefit—and there aren't many—of when I used to take the Long Island Railroad, was that the train never stunk like rotting dead fish. Occasionally, a person would smell like dead fish, but that was few and far between. Sure, there were always delays whether it was raining, snowing, or nothing but sun-shine. Sure, trains were canceled for unknown reasons. Sure, there was a suicidal jumper every month or so, but rotting fish, no.

The thing is; once you sit down for a few minutes, you actually get used to the torrid stench. Then, you get the ultimate pleasure of viewing all of the other passengers walk onto the train car and grimace with disgust. Now that is pure entertainment indeed.

Activate Your Inner Chuck Norris

Aren't we all looking for a little motivation from time to time—that friendly kick in the butt to get us going again after a long (or short) period of feeling sorry for ourselves, or simply not getting things done? Hell yeah we do.

We have all been at the point where we just can't get ourselves to go on, where we need some help and support from the outside, some positive reinforcement, some rush of positive energy, and there is no excuse whatsoever for making fun of people who are actively trying to get out. Get out of that swamp of laziness and procrastination to start following their goals and dreams again. NO EXCUSE!

Well . . . today I took a decently long subway ride during my lunch break and there was this one person who really put my good intentions of respectfully acknowledging this strive for motivation to the test. Because—it's pretty damn hard not to burst out laughing when the guy next to you on the subway in the deepest voice I have ever heard in my entire life and with a passion exceeding that of any talent casting show participant LOUDLY repeats motivational quotes like:

"You are not weak."

"You can do this."

"I am worthy."

"Work hard, dream big."

"Never settle for average."

"Make today ridiculously amazing."

"YOU ARE CHUCK NORRIS!"

Now, for those of you questioning, "come on, did this actually really happen?", the answer is YES. This actually happened and on top of that he was also fervently jotting down copious notes in a smaller than average-sized notebook.

He was so totally into it that he was completely oblivious to everything that started going on around him. On the seats behind him a group of four teenage boys had already started imitating him and were repeating the quotes after him. A man sitting next to me whipped out his cell phone and jotted down a few key one-liners. Waves of motivation were basically floating throughout the entire train.

One part of me, the part that was not almost lying on the floor, laughing hysterically, just wanted to go over to wanna-be-Chuck, give him a good tap on the shoulder and say "Way to go Mr. Norris. Way to go." But then again, there was this other part of me that just couldn't deal with the ridiculousness of the situation.

The fact that this man was wearing two different shoes and only ONE sock wasn't helping either. Just when I thought things couldn't possibly get any weirder, an elderly man walked up to 'Chuck 2.0' and sat down next to him.

"You know, back when I was your age, we didn't need any stupid stuff like this to motivate us. We had our hands, we had our work to do, that was all we needed. We built this country. You kids these days," (mind you this "kid" was about 45) "need all this hocus pocus, jibber jabber, to motivate you to get up off your lazy young ass and move it to the next Burger King to buy some good-for-nothing burger and fries."

To give his words even more depth, he waved his walking stick in front of Chuck's face. Unfortunately, by the time Chuck took off his headphones to see what all the commotion was, it was way too late for him to truly appreciate the immensity and deep meaning of this old man's short speech. Which was probably just as well since his self-esteem didn't appear to be that high to begin with. But the rest of us passengers on the train got the message. We heard it loud and clear, and that message was— thank you Chuck, thank you—you have just made our day ridiculously amazing.

Kim Kardashian

It's Wednesday and I am already feeling like it should be Friday. Just one of those weeks that seems to be taking FOREVER. We are now in July and today it is about 90 degrees outside. Now, I am not complaining since we had an extremely long, cold and harsh NYC winter but today on one of the hottest days of the year thus far, guess what happened on my commute home. Yep, you guessed it—NO AIR CONDITIONER and yes of course I am sandwiched between two larger-than-normal-sized individuals. To top it off, my boyfriend and I drank a little too much wine last night so the entire very long, long day has been an utter struggle. I wasn't looking like myself today; I was tired and out of it and had very little makeup on, just a bit of mascara left from the night before. So you can imagine my appearance after sweating like a beast for a full hour on my commute home.

After what felt like longer than an hour long commute today, my stop finally arrives and I stand in line with the other commuters to exit. Right when I stand up, a man sitting in the seat in front of mine taps me on the leg. So I said, "Yes?"

He goes, "Oh my goodness you look JUST like Kim Kardashian. Can I get your autograph?"

Admiring his choice of pickup line, I laugh it off and say thank you. But he persists and says, "No, really can I please have your autograph—you look just like her"

Mind you, I am a sweaty mess with only a smear of makeup on from the night before. Again I laugh it off and wish that the train doors would open already.

He then continues, "Please, please let me have your autograph, I want to remember this day—the day I met Kim Kardashian!"

At this point it was no longer flattering it was just creepy. Luckily a gentlemen standing behind me, also waiting to exit, got involved and said, "Sir, she isn't giving you her autograph." The doors magically opened and I was set free to step into my very non-Kim Kardashian-style apartment.

Weird and creepy—yes, however the strangest bit was the next day when I got into work bright and early and the head of HR stopped by my desk to ask me some unimportant question.

At the end of the conversation she said, "You know, you look a lot like someone famous, but I can't quite put my finger on it . . . ah, yes. It just came to me! You look just like Kim Kardashian!"

I'm still trying to figure out whether I should feel good now, or horrified.

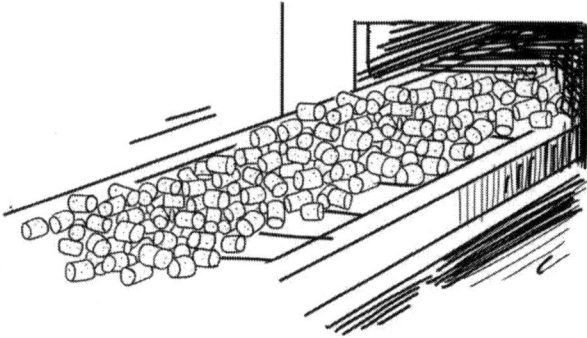

Marshmallow Madness

Today on my commute home, I learned that men gossip just as much as women do. Two men in their late 30s sat near me. They were tanned, dressed to the nines, with their black hair slicked all the way back, and I would have bet my life that they were investment bankers. Shortly after sitting down the mud-slinging and whining began. To my total shock, not only were the men not investment bankers but one of them actually works at the corporate office for a marshmallow producing company. He started venting to his buddy about how it was another rough day at the office and how they have to REALLY crack down on the number of marshmallows going MIA. I tried not to lose it when I heard this.

It seems that the mini-marshmallow department is culpable for the most "missing" spongy white delectable treats. These folks are eating 9% of the inventory and he is in charge of getting that number down to 5% or lower.

He said he has installed cameras but those "little piglets" keep consuming them. Then, he had the bright idea of having a person actually look at what was filmed. Now, there is a genius! Right there, that is book-smart stuff. Another idea he spoke of was to get rid of the hot chocolate machine. Apparently that thing is evil.

He went on to tell his buddy that he was messing around with the office manager's daughter. He doesn't like her, in fact he can't stand her, but he just wanted to irritate the guy. The father doesn't know about it, so how could this irritate him? He is actually torturing himself.

Then, he said that Anne, the secretary is dating two people from the mailroom—one male mailroom worker, and one female mailroom worker. That same secretary has been working late two or three times a week just so she can steal cases of water, K-cup coffee, sugar, and other break room items. And the IT guy has been stealing computers from the office and selling them on Craigslist.

I couldn't believe all of this could really be happening at one company and oh, there was much more, but you get the picture. Suddenly, my company didn't seem quite the madhouse that I had thought it was. Sure, my co-worker Jenny sings the theme song from Sesame Street all day. George the janitor spends 5 minutes cleaning the men's room, and 45 minutes cleaning the ladies' room. My boss loves eating jelly beans but eats only the green jellybeans and gives the rest to the staff. Karen, who is in the office across from me, counts the number of steps she takes out loud wherever she goes. When she goes to the break room, I find myself counting along with her.

However, this all seems quite normal to me now.

Married Man Train Breakup

Love ain't easy. Not being a teenager anymore and having spent a fair amount of time on this planet, I guess one of the most valuable lessons I've learned is love ain't easy. It never is. It's never like those dream-like scenarios we get served by literally EVERY TV-series EVER produced. It's never simple; it's never casual. There's always some kind of twist to it. But no matter how rough love may be on you, that's still nothing compared to Sally.

Trust me, Sally does have a harder time than you do. But let me start at the beginning, on a rainy evening on the train back home from work. To be honest, it hadn't been the easiest or happiest day for me either. A few things didn't go right at work and I wasn't sure if they were fixable, or whether I had to start over a project I had been working on for months completely from scratch. In short, I wasn't on top of things myself. But as soon as I sat down on the only available seat left, life taught me a lesson about how much worse things could be by presenting Sally; a blond, quite pretty girl in her late 20s, wearing way-too-red lipstick with way-too-little concealer to cover the dark circles under her eyes. But I got it. It was late. I was tired too. I quietly saluted my dark eye circled sister and just wanted to close my eyes to take a short half-awake-but-almost-asleep-nap when Sally decided to ruin those plans of mine by pulling out her iPhone and starting a conversation with, quote, "Dannyyyyyyyyyy darling."

Due to the volume of her voice, it was impossible to zone out, so I accepted my fate and started to pay attention. Little did I know, oh-so little. Turns out Sally was actually about to initiate a break up, but not your regular "girl decides that her boyfriend is far from what she had expected" kinda breakup. This one was quite special. Because Sally's 'prince' actually was a married man in his 40s. Yes, ladies and gentlemen. Sally might be one of the very few people having to go through the struggle of breaking up with a man who's married to another woman; a quite delicate situation. Also, Sally turned out to be a rather emotional human being. After listening for just a few minutes, I basically knew everything about

68

this girl's life, even the name of her recently deceased hamster Jarred. May he rest in peace.

The amount of random facts she managed to incorporate into a breakup conversation ON THE PHONE, ON A TRAIN, surrounded by strangers who either did or didn't pretend to listen amazed me. Turns out, *Dannyyyyyyyyyy* didn't take it all that well. I could hear him crying desperately through the phone and I couldn't help but feel a bit sorry for him. Poor, cheating, lying Danny got his heart broken on the 8pm train.

"I just don't see a future for us, hun. You're not getting any younger you know." Sally really knew how to crush the man, stabbing right into his 40+ year old heart. "It was good while it lasted, really, but . . . I kinda moved on. And so should you. At least you still got Sandra!"

Oh yeah, why not take the pity prize aka *the wife*. I mean, if the young affair lets you down, ain't no shame in going for the next best option—which in this case literally was the NEXT best option, assuming that *Dannyyyyyyyyyy's* wife was somewhere close by.

It was surreal. Judging from the continuing weeping sounds coming through the speaker, Danny wasn't too happy with this option. The man obviously had other plans. And sexy, lipstick-wearing Sally, for sure, would have been a way-too-young part of those plans. But train rides can be cruel; they can be revealing, life changing, merciless. Danny had to experience that first hand, as did the passengers being live witnesses to Sally breaking her married boyfriend's heart.

After what felt like an eternity of crying, emotions and random hamster facts, Sally finally decided that she had spent enough time making a grown man cry and hung up with a half-hearted, "See ya, hun." Maybe at that point even Danny realized that dating a woman like Sally probably wasn't the best idea of his married life. Or maybe he didn't. Maybe Sally would actually date a single guy next, or maybe she wouldn't. Love—it ain't easy.

Party All Morning Long!

As I sit down on my favorite seat, in my favorite train car and sip my coffee, I stare at everyone around me looking like a misery, and I realize what the true problem is here; I realize why we are all miserable during our morning commute. The problem with coffee in the morning is that there is no alcohol in it. Just imagine how much better your morning would be if there were two shots of your favorite liquor in there. Instead of everyone looking and feeling like miserable cogs in a wheel, everyone would be chipper and ready to take on the day!

That nonsensical jibber jabber you encounter every morning with the world's most boring receptionist suddenly becomes big fun and, to your surprise, even enjoyable. The coffee pot in the pantry is empty and typically cuss words would be flying out of your mouth, but not this day. Now when you have to waste ten minutes making a new pot, it is suddenly a joyous event. It's a delightful task now, and it even gives you extra time to make random small talk with people that you know you hate. Today, however, you don't hate them quite as much—everyone is your friend today! Well except for Ashley—there are some things *even alcohol* can't change.

The boss gives you an urgent project on top of your already impossible workload. The response in your head is, "Is that all you got? Bring it on!"

Just imagine the endless possibilities if your first morning cup of coffee had those two secret shots in there. How riveting your morning meetings would become! Instead of nodding off per usual, your mind runs wildly amuck. Your droll boss seems to make less sense than ever, but today it is rather amusing. In fact, you struggle to hold back the chuckles and laughter. To fight these urges, you picture your boss with no clothes on. Yep, that quickly quells any bit of fun.

Well now, that was a nice random daydream for 7:29 in the morning. Oh well, back to enjoying my boring straight-laced cup of coffee—until happy hour that is!

Thankful for Shoes

Have you ever taken a moment to really appreciate your shoes? I mean, every day we walk around the most disgusting places and if it weren't for those wonderful rubber barriers between your bare feet and the icky ground, our nice clean feet would be touching that icky ground! To be honest I don't know how many people have really given the shoe much thought or much thanks! Sure, there are all types of different shoes and especially we ladies love to collect such things and may have dozens of pairs of shoes in the closet; but we really don't appreciate the veritable necessity of them.

The heat was barely working on the train on this cold February morning, but I seemed to have avoided frostbite on any of my extremities. I looked down at my shoes and wondered what life would be without them. I thought to myself, life would be very, very bad without them! What a luxury being able to wear shoes is, yet we all go through our everyday life not giving them a second thought—unless the thought is *brown or black*? Or, *do these shoes match my outfit?*

As I sat on the train pondering my shoes' existence, I started wondering if there were any other souls on the entire train who were thinking about and appreciating their shoes at that very moment. Sadly, I tend to think not. Most likely, it's just strange ol' me. I either have a very creative mind or I have too much time on my hands—commute time. Most people are reading the paper, thinking about real world problems, looking at the stock market or thinking about their to-do lists. They are definitely not consumed by the brilliant invention of the shoe.

Every morning I take the same route through Grand Central and every morning I pass the shoe shine stand which always has a long line of folks waiting for their shoes to get a makeover. This morning was no different, and I thought to myself how mind boggling it is that people would even bother to get their shoes shined in the dead of winter. As soon as they are finished with their footwear rubdown, they step right in the snowy, slushy, salt-laden sidewalk—

which again, really made me appreciate the luxury of the shoe! I can't stand the thought of how grotesque it would be walking around NYC with bare feet!

Each day is truly a great day to be thankful for the shoe, especially if you have ever taken the time to look down to witness what you are actually stepping in. That is today's train thought of the day folks! I hope I have enlightened you.

It is a Man's World . . . or *Is It*?

Taking the subway during rush hour in August is always fun . . . that is, if you're into hot, sweaty and uncomfortable experiences. The subway becomes a stifling sweat box during these times and finding a free seat is pretty much a godsend. Feeling lucky to have snagged one, I was sitting there sweaty but happy when a strong, invincible, hulk-like creature squeezed into the sliver of space next to me. After maneuvering himself into a spot much too small for his much too large body, he proceeded to spread his legs SO wide, because HELL YEAH, HE CAN. For the rest of the journey, I watched the space in between his legs get wider and wider as I was rammed further and further into the metal pole. And I started thinking what it would be like—

growing a beard, drinking endless amounts of beer, watching football on Sunday afternoons and constantly scratching inappropriate places. In case I didn't make myself clear enough, I am talking about what it would be like to be a MAN.

Before anyone gets upset, I know that most of the above mentioned are stereotypical assumptions, but wouldn't it be fun, ladies, to walk in "male shoes" for—let's say, a day? Who knows what kind of a guy I would be. Maybe the knight in shining armor I always dreamed about; always prepared to rescue his damsel in distress—or maybe not. Maybe I would be THAT guy (yeah, we all know him), walking the streets feeling too damn good about himself and annoying everyone with his overly expressed masculinity (or what he believes to be masculinity).

One thing I know for sure. My name would be John. Yeah, that's what every guy is called, but hey, I like the name and I feel like it suits me . . . him. Whatever. So what would *John* do? I just realized this is starting to sound like the title to some self-help TV show for teenage boys. Anyway, John would definitely follow his passion in life. John would not let anyone tell him how to go about things, how to walk, talk and act. John would be confident. But wait. Is it possible that John would actually kinda be like . . . me?

Maybe being a man wouldn't actually change me that much. At least not in the way I behave, feel and express myself. But it would change a lot when it comes to how others perceive me. Because isn't it all about perception in the end? God, this is getting way too philosophical, let's get back on track here, people, because *John* is definitely thirsty and about to go grab his can of ice cold beer. Or two. Or maybe even three. And we all know John, in fact, needs these cans of beer. Because when you think about it, life isn't that easy for men after all. You have to find that fine line between being an egotistic macho jerk who treats women like nice accessories (at best) and being the understanding, sensitive Mister-nice-guy who stands in front of your door with a box of chocolates and some wine if his girl is feeling down.

Men are expected to be tough, but sensible, strong, but caring; the hero and the villain in just one person. Contemplating all of this, I guess I'm sticking to worrying about finding a well-fitting bra that doesn't make my boobs disappear in some 'bra-parallel-universe', about matching my shoes and handbag, about bad hair days and too much humidity. Because even if those problems may seem ridiculous at times . . . I still kind of like the female struggle. This doesn't mean that John won't always have a place in the back of my mind, and if I feel like it, I'll grab myself those cans of beer. Because not only HE—but also, I CAN.

Train in Vain

When I'm sitting on the train relaxing after work, I start thinking about the things I need to do or the people I need to get back to outside of my day job world. Either I have been putting these things off on purpose, or I just haven't been in the mood for them. Or maybe I just haven't had the time. Or, because these tasks and people irritate the shit out of me.

Besides my day job, which always consumes the best parts of the day, I have a jewelry company called New Age Charm. It's about one million dollars short of a million-dollar business. It's a jewelry company that pairs meaningful symbols with semi-precious stones. Each piece of jewelry has a unique meaning, which is meant to empower the wearer in their everyday life.

Since I do have a full time job (and for those curious to what that is—I work at an international mid-sized company, planning exclusive events for our board members) and I cannot yet support myself on my side business, a lot of my creative thinking happens on my train ride home. Not so much happens on my commute in because I am only semi-coherent in the morning and I barely have enough energy to raise the coffee mug to my face. As my younger sister would say, "The struggle is real."

But, back to the main point of this entry; I have been trying to get pricing from different places on molds for pieces of jewelry. For those not familiar with how jewelry is made, a mold is first required and then the piece needs to be casted in whatever metal you are working with.

So, I messaged a person I met in the midtown Jewelry District to give me pricing on a Hamsa mold in sterling silver. The Hamsa symbol means *hand of protection*. It starts off normal, and he says "Well, first I design the 3D CAD model then I make the mold and I'll charge you $250 for that."

That made sense, so I proceeded to ask, "Okay, after that, how much is it per piece in sterling silver?" My question was ignored and he said, "It's all based on weight." Yeah, so is Jenny Craig, but I wanted a price!

So I said, "Right, I understand that, but let's say I order 50 pieces of this size and it's about 4 grams per piece. Approximately how much would it be?" My question was circumvented, and instead he answered the other question that I asked him previously.

I was annoyed because I just couldn't get a straightforward price. He gave me the run around and we went back and forth for, I would say, two hours of train time. So finally I said, "Yeah, I get that the mold is $250, but how much would it be if I got 50 pieces of this?"

Well, the answer I got next was . . . umm, *again* not addressing what was asked. "After casting, you need a jeweler to clean the castings, then a polisher to polish and a plater to plate the jewelry." He proceeded to follow up with, "I hope I answered all your questions! Let me know if you need anything further."

After reading that, I had an incredible urge to poke this person in the eyes. I thought to myself— "How about removing your foot from your ass and answering the damn question!"

Lord, have mercy on my soul. I felt like an idiot for asking once again. It was turning into something of a Seinfeld episode, but I still didn't have my answer. So, here we go again, "How much would 50 pieces of the Hamsa cost, Goddammit?!!"

This should not be rocket science. At that moment, I made a silent blessing for the sangria that I had the foresight to buy prior to boarding the train. Oh, thank goodness for sangria and F— the hand of protection. Now, exactly where did I put that giant straw I purchased?

Pondering Life at 2:00 am

There's something especially philosophical about sitting on the train going home at 2am after having drowned all the sorrows of your existence in what you remember as being about four Cosmopolitans and an unknown amount of white wine. It's like the overly used seats and dirty windows scream: THINK ABOUT YOUR LIFE! So yeah, that's exactly what I did last Friday night . . . Saturday morning . . . whatever, you know what I mean.

As for me, exactly what I did was count my blessings. And by 'blessings' I mean getting out of bad dating choices. And by 'bad dating choices' I mean A-holes that I met time and time again after being tricked into first dates by their fancy and well put together profile pages on dating websites. Now, breathing in the slightly stuffy train air, they all appeared right in front of my inner eye.

David, the guy with the body of a Greek god and the intellect of a cobblestone—David, with whom every conversation drifted off within only a few seconds to a very select choice of topics including sports, himself, sports and him doing sports. David, who couldn't utter a grammatically correct sentence but— OH BOY, those abs . . . seriously, those abs were from another planet. Well, after the initial pleasure of admiring his shredded physique, I quickly realized I would be having a better time conversing with that painted wall behind me. At least it would listen.

Then, there was Mike. Mike was what I would describe as the exact opposite of his ripped predecessor. Mike was intelligent, witty, had so many degrees that at some point I simply stopped counting, and whenever I told people about him, I stuck to saying: "He's got brains, you know." This guy satisfied my intellectual needs in a man. We had endless talks until the early morning hours. We discussed everything from the meaning of life to how meaningless life was. At least talking to each other was what I thought we did. In retrospect, it was more like Mike conducted extensive monologues which I more or less coincidentally happened to witness. Lucky me.

Then we had Jay, the guy who scheduled a U-Haul rental truck on the first date because he was positive he had met the *one* . . .

So here I was, sitting on this strange-smelling train, going back further and further in my dating history, starting to question if I was simply destined to end up unlucky in love. Maybe I should abstain from men for good. Who needs them anyway? Like—I am an independent woman, I can handle things just fine on my own. . . I don't need anyone . . . I can . . . Oh, hey there cutie pie on the seat in front of me. Didn't see you there. You look exactly like what I need right now.

Ham or Not, That is the Question

I would say that morning is my enemy. It takes away my sleep, forces me to go to work, and, worst of all, it makes me listen to all of the conversations that go on in the train. Don't get me wrong, there are various conversations to choose from, but usually the quality is rather low.

There I was, leaning on the metal pole, trying to stay awake while the train was lulling me back to sleep. Two indistinctive figures were sitting across from me and they were strangers to one another, just as I was to them. I chose to look at them because they seemed so peaceful and soothing, something I really needed.

Then it happened. The man sitting on the right made a horrible mistake, one I could not forgive, and it all began. He took out a ham sandwich and before he could grab that first, most satisfying bite, he was interrupted by the unexpectedly high-pitched voice of the man on the left.

"Are you insane?"

The man on the right closed his mouth and slowly turned around.

"Excuse me?"

"I can smell the ham in your sandwich from here. If you're eating garbage food, at least have the decency to think about us healthy vegetarians."

The man on the right became infuriated and put the sandwich down but continued to argue. The man on the left argued back, and after a minute or two it became a true word fight. I could feel them stomping on my brain. It got so heated that at one point the sandwich ended up on the floor, smudged all around. I couldn't help but notice how I felt like that sandwich.

The Creeper

It was morning again, and quite a difficult one. When the alarm clock started yelling at me, I hid under the blankets and pretended not to hear it.

Sleepwalking, I stepped onto the train and nearly hit the window on the way in. *Who put that there?* The train was as empty as my head at that moment and I couldn't care less. My eyes swayed downward to my watch and in some sort of small horror I realized the train was running late. *Great,* I thought, and looked angrily in the direction of the man driving this screeching solid box.

Instead of punishing the train operator with an unforgiving look, I somehow attracted the unwanted gaze of a peculiar-looking gentleman three feet away. I quickly shifted my gaze to pretend I wasn't looking directly at him and turned in the opposite direction to find a seat. Settling into the routine of my morning commute, I put my headphones on and took a few sips of my coffee. Drifting off into the majestic land of my iPhone playlist, my eyes were shutting and I was feeling at peace.

Unfortunately, the peace did not last because I was rudely awakened 15 minutes later by someone pulling an earphone out of my ear. Then came a whisper, "Hi beautiful, my name is Sam." Startled, I woke up and realized this was the same gentleman I had made accidental eye contact with earlier. I thought to myself, *just* what I need to deal with in the morning . . . a train suitor. Trying to be polite, I said "Nice to meet you, have a great day," put my earphones back in and stared out the window trying to pretend he was no longer sitting in front of me.

Again he reached over and pulled my earphone out! "Sorry to bother you, but can I take you to dinner tonight?"

Ugh, I thought. I was in no mood to be courted—go away! Woman commuters don't have it easy; you have to deal with men hitting on you when you are just minding your own business. I told him "Sorry I am already in a serious relationship."

Instead of doing what a normal person would do, which is to walk away; he just sat there the entire train ride STARING at me. I could feel his eyes fixated on me the entire trip. I would have moved but it was a packed car and I didn't feel like standing, so I pretended not to notice him. We were starting to approach Grand Central and I was thrilled I would soon be able to escape from his uncomfortable stare.

About five minutes prior to exiting, I see him take out his iPhone . . . and I thought, *oh good,* he got bored of looking at me for the past hour. But no, that wasn't quite it. By the way he was angling his iPhone, I could tell he was snapping photos of me! Clearly that was the last straw! I popped up and walked to a different train car.

About 3 months later, I was nearing my stop when a man sat down and tapped my leg and said, "Hey, hey you look incredibly familiar; do I know you?"

At first I didn't recognize him, but then I realized it was SAM. I said, "No, no, I don't think I know you."

He goes, "It's weird because I have a picture on my phone of a girl that looks exactly like you. I must know you from somewhere!"

It just doesn't get creepier than that folks!

Just One of Those PB-and-Jelly Kinda Days . . .

I love taking the subway in NYC. Seriously, I really do. It's always like a small adventure; you never know which people you are about to meet, which absurdly comical situation you'll find yourself in and which more or less heroic action you may have the honor of witnessing. Usually the stuff I see is less on the heroic side of things. Like 'PB-and-Jelly-Tie Guy'.

For the sake of practicality, let's call him Fred. Fred was sitting next to me on the subway just yesterday and, *oh Lord*, Fred seemed to be having an even worse day than I was. I'm not sure if I'm the only one who does this, but I tend to create stories around people I meet. They are not just anonymous faces; they are literally moving stories to me. And so was Fred.

I have to say, I felt a little sorry for him, sitting there with his tie covered in what looked like the sad remains of what used to be his breakfast, and a look on his face both confused and slightly lost. I felt the strong desire to hug the poor guy and say, "We all have those days Fred. It's gonna be alright."

Life sucked for Fred on this particular day. He should have known things were about to go downhill when the night before he, once again, offered moral support to Jane (his best friend and not-so-secret crush since kindergarten who had friend-zoned him from the moment they first met and he flubbed his first "Hello" to her). Approximately five boxes of chocolate and an uncountable amount of tissues handed by him to the sobbing and weeping Jane later, she ended up throwing him out. After all, she needed time for herself—to think about things and to figure out how to get back 'Mister If-I-workout-just-a-little-more-you-might-break-something-touching-my-body'. So Fred ended up back at his highly overpriced apartment, downing a bottle of red wine of unknown origin that he to his own surprise had found in the back of his fridge. Cheers to good friends and ripped abs.

Not so surprisingly at all, the next morning was a rather rough one for Fred. There are so many kinds of headaches. There's the bumping ones, the pulsating ones, the ones that go all the way down the back of your skull and even further down your spine. Fred had the PLEASE-LORD-LET-ME-DIE kinda one—which is especially cruel if you are hung-over and hungry at the same time, which means you are both craving food and highly disgusted by the thought of it entering your mouth. I like to call this state 'sungry'—sick and hungry.

Only God knows how Fred managed to prepare himself the peanut butter and jelly sandwich that would later on decorate his tie in a very unique way. But he did. He stood his man. Fred was a damn HERO that morning. Because regardless of all the humiliation and hopelessness of his never-ending love for Jane who obviously preferred guys who treated her like garbage as long as their bodies resembled the ones you find in those annoying fitness magazines. Regardless of all that, FRED MADE THAT SANDWICH. So who was I to judge him for looking like a lost school boy sitting on the subway with his breakfast all over himself? You know what, I felt with Fred. And I couldn't help but salute him before leaving the train. You go Fred. We all have those days.

The Guilt Trip

We live in an unforgiving world where everything costs something. If you want to eat, you have to pay; if you want to drink you have to pay; and, of course, if you want to ride the Metro-North train, guess what? Yes, you have to pay! It was early Monday morning and coming off a long weekend with friends, my mind was not quite in work mode yet.

When I entered the train everything was great, but the second the doors closed a thought came into my useless head—*ugh*, I left my monthly ticket in my other bag! For those of you not familiar with the costs of the Metro North, it's about $300 for a monthly pass, but if you forget it and have to pay for a roundtrip ticket on the train it's about $20. Now that's $20 on top of the $300, so as you can imagine it is quite an annoying additional expense for something you already paid for, and in my mind is way too expensive to begin with.

Annoyed with myself, there was nothing I could do but wait, wait for my turn for the pesky ticket collector to come around. In the meantime I try to muster up some excuse to where I think he or she may give me a pass. So it begins . . . the terrible anxiety of preparing your speech for the ticket conductor. You begin reciting your story to yourself over and over again preparing for your grand reveal. Panic began crawling inside every part of my body. Will he/she accept my sorry excuse for forgetting my ticket or will I have to pay up. I continue to recite my most plausible excuses and anxiously await my big moment.

Then it happened; he appeared in a train car down from me clicking his way up the line, and I heard the dreaded sound—*Tickets, please!*

About ten people between us, I knew it was time to think fast. Perhaps I could think of some good reason why I didn't have a ticket? Let's see.

Dog ate my ticket.
Where's YOUR ticket?
I already gave you my ticket.
What is this "ticket" you speak of?

No, thank you!

It's OK, I am the conductor.

Show me yours and I'll show you mine!

THAT man told me I didn't need a ticket!

Tickets, please!

I could hear his sonorous voice draw near. I looked at him, studied him to find a weak spot. He was an older man, quite unimpressive in every way, with a deadpan facial expression. I knew I was done.

Tickets, please!

Perhaps if I sit somewhere else or walk behind him, he wouldn't notice? Maybe I can jump out of the window and hold on to the train Hollywood-style? Maybe I can play dumb? Huh? *Play?*

Tickets, please!

He was right in front of me now. I turned white and started rummaging through my empty purse pretending like I would find something in there. I looked up to meet his eyes. It was time to come clean. As my eyes made contact with his, I heard ...

"Thank you!"

Thank you? What happened? I looked at him and I realized he was actually asking the woman sitting next to me. He inadvertently skipped me all together. I stepped off of the train feeling like I had won the lottery.

Stomp the Beat

You know, in general I have nothing against old people. Some of them are really quite sweet, like the lady living right down my street. She always smiles at me and has something nice to say when we meet. "You look lovely today sweetheart! What a wonderful blouse you're wearing today!" Stuff like that. And yes, I appreciate compliments, even if they are coming from a lady who's in her 80s. Rough times guys, rough times . . .

Anyway, back to what I wanted to tell you. Not all of our elderly folk are quite that nice to be around. Like grumpy old 'Cane Guy' I met on the train yesterday. He for sure wasn't part of the nice-grandpa-club. They probably kicked him out the first day he tried to get in. He was sitting in an aisle seat when I entered the train, his walking cane in his hands, looking like he was angry at the world. I mean, I get it, it was Monday evening. It was unbearably hot on the train. There was no AC, *again* (at some point sweat just becomes something like a fashion accessory on train rides) and people were especially rude and well, they were just . . . existing—which kinda was already enough to begin with.

My point is, being grumpy was an understandable emotional state to be in on such a day. But 'Cane Guy' took being grumpy to a whole new level. Every time a passenger entered what felt like either hell or some weird fully clothed sauna, he stared at them with a look so full of general disgust that I couldn't help but be amazed by the intensity of his hatred for others, and he started banging his walking stick on the floor. Not once, not twice, SEVERAL TIMES.

The whole thing was completely ridiculous since he was dead silent when the train was in motion and started up his weird cane stomping again when it stopped at a station. People were irritated to say the least, and so was I. After the first few stations, in order to deal with this, I started playing this game with myself where I tried humming a matching melody in my head.

...Weee will (STOMP), weee will (STOMP), rock you (STOMP, STOMP), rock you (STOMP, STOMP)...

Cane Guy and I really got in the rhythm of things, literally. While all the other people on the train got more and more upset about the constant cane banging and intense staring, I started enjoying it more and more. If only Cane Guy would have known he was the source of my joy on an awfully hot and otherwise boring train ride, maybe he would have stomped even harder out of pure frustration.

I was trying to fit Madonna's *Like a Virgin* into the stomping beat, when a woman in a very expensive dress totally lost it. It came out of nowhere, no warning signs, but this lady obviously had had enough.

With make-up running down her face from sweating, she got up from her seat, walked over to the old man and screamed "For Christ's sake, sir, can you please do all of us a favor and stop this brain-damaging stomping. You're driving everyone crazy!"

Cane Guy pulled the, *'I'm just gonna ignore you and see what you can do about that'* card and didn't even look at her. Not only was he angry. He was badass. He was the Clint Eastwood of the Monday evening train. Only he toted a cane instead of a gun—but not a bit less intimidating. This guy knew it was his God given right to freakin' stomp his cane and Lord

101

knows, that's what he did. The well-dressed woman eventually gave up, accepting her defeat and all the other passengers sat there, helpless, like scared children.

I couldn't help but feel amused. When the next stop came, everybody's eyes turned on Cane Guy. Would he? Or wouldn't he? You could feel the tension in the boiling air. The train slowed down, could it really be that this time he wouldn't . . .

...Stop! (STOMP, STOMP) in the naaame of love (STOMP, STOMP), before you break (STOMP) my heart (STOMP, STOMP)...

The Amazing Sauerkraut

No one ever mentions this, but it is my fervent belief that there should always be some entertainment during daily commuting. The railways should hire someone who will be the designated entertainer— someone who will make sure the passengers start their day with a smile, or at least a grin. I like that idea very much (even though it seems logical because it's mine).

Thankfully today, my entertainment prayers were answered in the form of a small brunette with an exceptional sense for situational comedy. She appeared before my eyes, sat right across from me and with a couple of feverish looks around took out her foil-wrapped treasure.

The woman seemed quite ordinary, perhaps even too ordinary! That is what made it so funny, I guess. She was elegant, clean and perfect in almost every sense. The only thing that stood out was the fact that she was holding a massive hot dog in her hands. Hunger strikes us all, what can be done? The look in her eyes when she uncovered that unhealthy, steaming delight smothered with mustard and sauerkraut was priceless. She looked at it as if a wild beast silently waited inside of her. Before I could even realize what happened, she dove into the hot dog and took a massive, savage bite.

That bite satisfied her wild cravings for a while and I could see that she thought she got away with it. What made me smile, however, was the huge chunk of sauerkraut that got stuck up her nose without her knowledge. In the next moment as she was preparing for bite number two, the chunk of sauerkraut in her nose decided to change its residence and returned back to her hot dog. Instantly, horror overcame her.

Where did it come from? How? Why? What year, month? Hellooo? Is this REAL LIFE?!

I could see she was beginning to lose her mind as she started looking at the train ceiling for clues. After a while of searching, it seemed she gave up on finding out where the sauerkraut had fallen from and hunger took over again. She looked all around the train to make sure there were no witnesses. Of course I looked away; I am quite skillful when it comes to these things, and she continued engorging herself.

If no one saw it, it didn't happen.

When the train reached my station, I stepped out as fast as I could and once I was far enough away, I burst out laughing for about five minutes straight. I don't think I will be able to look at sauerkraut in the same way again . . . *ever*.

Modern Mona Lisa

Beauty lies in the eye of the beholder. This sounds like a cheesy thing to say, but guess what—it's true. It was Friday night and I was on my way home after happy hour involving maybe one or two margaritas too many (it's Matt's fault; he's my favorite bartender and, *MAN,* I can tell you, his cocktails are equally delicious and mean . . . let's just say Matt has saved quite a few seemingly unsavable evenings). So there I was, sitting on the train, humming a Tina Turner song in my head, minding my own business, when two guys in their late 20s (or early 30s, as you can never really tell these days) sat down on the free seats opposite me. They looked like they had, like me, enjoyed one or two or three alcoholic beverages over the course of the evening and were busy talking about their female conquests of the night.

Well actually, one of them was talking and the other dude just listened, while throwing in a few "Oh wow, that's awesome" and "Daaaaaamn, man" here and there. Talkative guy (let's call him *Dan* for the sake of this story) kept on rambling about how (quote:) "freakin' hot" mystery woman was and how lucky he felt that she considered him worth spending her precious time with. I was rather unimpressed. After a ten-minute-long detailed description of the way she drank her gin tonic (I may have zoned out for some time to be honest), Dan had managed to get his friend interested enough to ask questions about her looks. That was where I checked myself back into the conversation. It's irrationally interesting to me to hear how men evaluate female appearance. I always feel like some researcher, exploring the behavior of some newly discovered species, *The Male*, in its natural habitat (a smelly train, in my case).

"I don't know man, she was just so hot. I can't even . . . just hot, you know?" Dan wasn't a man of big words but he sure was a man of many small words. "*Hot*, like . . . like some really hot chick, with *hair*, like . . . like some really sexy hair. And *eyes* . . . like, they were really pretty, you know?'"

Yeah, thanks Dan. We kinda got the idea. Just like me, Dan's friend didn't seem convinced. He tried to get a somewhat better description of the notorious unknown beauty but Dan, again, failed to deliver. I mean, I get it, in a way. I also can have a hard time describing people. And just like Dan's friend, people seem to get angry at me because of that. It's like I purposely deny them essential information without which they can't possibly sleep that night. Or ever. This combination of anger, frustration and desperation was what I sensed in the two men. They ended up going through all kinds of celebrities to eventually find a comparable lady among the endless amounts of more or less important people you find on TV screens and magazine pages, and on Twitter. Lord knows, they *ALL* are on Twitter. Apparently you can Twitter even if you don't have anything to say—anything at all. Quite astonishing, if you think about it.

But back to Dan and his wonder woman, who kept getting more and more mysterious as the train plodded along since she didn't seem to look the slightest bit like ANY of the female celebs Dan's friend mentioned. And trust me; he mentioned a lot of them.

"Come on man, she must look like SOMEONE after all, at least a little bit! Give me something to work with here!"

Dan was struggling, I could tell. I almost wanted to hand him a pen and paper and let him draw her just to relieve them both from their misery. But I didn't have a pen. Or paper. For Christ's sake, I didn't even have a mirror! In a way, I was angry at *Daniel* too. It was not fair of him to get us all excited and then leave us hanging like that. I felt personally invested in his relationship with the indescribable beauty and felt like I deserved more than just the unsatisfying information he could provide.

We were approaching my station and I was mentally preparing myself to leave the train without ever finding out what 'Ms. X' looked like when suddenly, out of nowhere, like a gunshot, Dan had a moment of enlightenment. "I got it! I got it! A Modern Mona Lisa! She looked like a freakin' Modern Mona Lisa, dude!" Both his friend and I were equally taken aback by that statement. He continued . . . "Wow man. Just . . . *WOW* . . . that's it! I freakin' got it—a Modern Mona Lisa."

His friend was at a loss for words, as was I. Although considered quite beautiful in her heyday, have you recently looked at a picture of that painting? . . . Yikes . . . not exactly what anyone would describe as beautiful in these modern times. But hey, I guess anyone can date someone looking like Jessica Alba or Jennifer Laurence. But seriously, Mona Lisa? It takes some serious gumption to take out a girl like that . . .

Train Hand

Trains are a funny thing. In a way, they make us interact with people, though sometimes more than we would really like. It is as if they feel we're not paying enough attention to each other so they cram us inside and makes us socialize. Yes, that's just what I need in the morning, before I've had my first coffee.

Sometimes I need to take the subway, and it's usually early in the morning. My eyes are half-open and my body is limp. In those moments I feel as if the wind could blow me away, and all I need is some peace of mind and possibly some quiet time.

On this particular day, I got on the train as usual. It was a bit colder than it should be but I didn't notice it that much. I felt like a sardine—completely immobile in this huge crowd of people. I could almost fall asleep while standing up. Then, all of a sudden, something happened. Someone's freezing hand touched mine and refused to move. I was shocked by the cold fingers that seemed to drain all the heat out of me. I looked at the man, but he pretended like nothing happened, smiled softly and still refused to move his hand. What was he thinking? Did he think this was a good way to meet somebody? Without buying me dinner first?

He got out of the train at the next station and nodded in my direction with an undefined grin. I stood there almost paralyzed, not knowing what just happened. Were we friends now? Acquaintances?

I decided to wear gloves in the future.

Conclusion

So here we are, at the end of my real life commuting tales and let me tell you, I actually feel closer to you now. I really do! The train I take every day to and from work plays a central role in my life and it feels so good to be sharing my experiences with you. The things I have experienced on that train made me laugh, some made me think and others made me almost cry— usually with laughter. But the most important thing is, they actually made me feel something. Emotions are too often downgraded and not appreciated enough in our modern society, so I am glad I have been able to share some of that with you. I never thought this past year of commuting would turn into a book, but I'm so glad it did. I hope you have enjoyed reading and reliving my experiences as much as I did writing them. Most of all I hope I made you laugh! And hopefully laugh on your commute somewhere to someplace.

It's my belief that every day is a gift and although we sometimes have to do unpleasant things during our days, I feel that the best can always be made out of it. The 480 hours I have spent commuting this past year hasn't been your typical commuting drudgery— it has been exciting and enjoyable. So if you enjoyed what you just read, please stay tuned for my new book which will be out in the coming months, *Texts My Mom Sends*. If you think I'm funny, my mom might actually take the cake. It will be comprised of her real life text messages to me coupled with my commentary. And as long as I'm still taking the train there will be plenty of incoming material to write a follow up series.

Additionally, if you enjoyed my stories that referenced my spiritual jewelry company and want to own a piece of enlightenment for yourself, you can find it online at:

NEW AGE CHARM   www.newagecharm.com

Thank you for taking the time to read this book. I look forward to more future journeys with you. And remember, sometimes it's not the big moments in life, that bring us the most joy. Sometimes it's the small ones—the ones that you experience every day, the moments that are often overlooked but that shouldn't be. Life should always be about laughter and fun no matter where you are or what you are doing. Take care until next time my friends!

16155165R00069

Printed in Poland
by Amazon Fulfillment
Poland Sp. z o.o., Wrocław